Why Is Today Cloudy and Gray?

Tracy Kompelien

Consulting Editor, Diane Craig, M.A./Reading Specialist

Published by ABDO Publishing Company, 4940 Viking Drive, Edina, Minnesota 55435.
Copyright © 2007 by Abdo Consulting Group, Inc. International copyrights reserved in all countries.
No part of this book may be reproduced in any form without written permission from the publisher.
SandCastle™ is a trademark and logo of ABDO Publishing Company.

Printed in the United States.

Credits
Edited by: Pam Price
Curriculum Coordinator: Nancy Tuminelly
Cover and Interior Design and Production: Mighty Media
Photo Credits: Shutterstock, Steve Wewerka

Library of Congress Cataloging-in-Publication Data
Kompelien, Tracy, 1975-
  Why is today cloudy and gray? / Tracy Kompelien.
     p. cm. -- (Synonyms)
  ISBN-13: 978-1-59928-732-4
  ISBN-10: 1-59928-732-3
  1. English language--Synonyms and antonyms--Juvenile literature. I. Title.

PE1591.K6574 2007
423'.12--dc22
                            2006031428

SandCastle™ books are created by a professional team of educators, reading specialists, and content developers around five essential components—phonemic awareness, phonics, vocabulary, text comprehension, and fluency—to assist young readers as they develop reading skills and strategies and increase their general knowledge. All books are written, reviewed, and leveled for guided reading, early reading intervention, and Accelerated Reader® programs for use in shared, guided, and independent reading and writing activities to support a balanced approach to literacy instruction.

Let Us Know

SandCastle would like to hear your stories about reading this book. What is your favorite page? Was there something hard that you needed help with? Share the ups and downs of learning to read. We want to hear from you! To get posted on the ABDO Publishing Company Web site, send us e-mail at:

sandcastle@abdopublishing.com

SandCastle Level: Fluent

A synonym is a word that has the same or a similar meaning as another word.

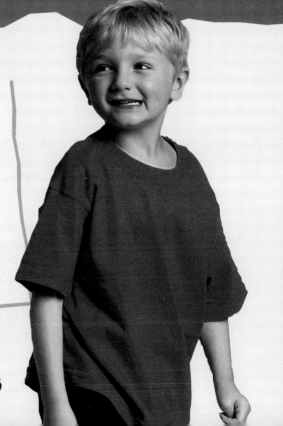

Here is a good way to remember what a synonym is:

synonym
=
same
=
similar

3

synonyms

It is a nice day.

pleasant

lovely

agreeable

pleasing

good

6

synonyms

The rainbow is colorful.

bright

vibrant

vivid

brilliant

synonyms

The sky is gloomy.

gray   cloudy

overcast

stormy   foggy

10

synonyms

It is cold and snowy in the winter.

freezing

chilly

cool

brisk

12

synonyms

Kim uses an umbrella on
wet days.

moist   damp

rainy

soggy

14

synonyms

Hanna does not like rainy days. She walks through soggy streets on the way to school. The damp drizzle makes her hair frizzy. Hanna prefers to be in the bright sun!

Can you find any synonyms for the word rainy in the paragraph above?

16

synonyms

It is a lovely day. The sun is high in the beautiful sky. The sun makes the temperature pleasant and warm. The sky is clear and bright.

Can you find any synonyms for the word lovely in the paragraph above?

17

synonyms

Seth likes to skate in the winter. When the weather turns chilly, the lake freezes. Seth enjoys skating in the brisk, cool air.

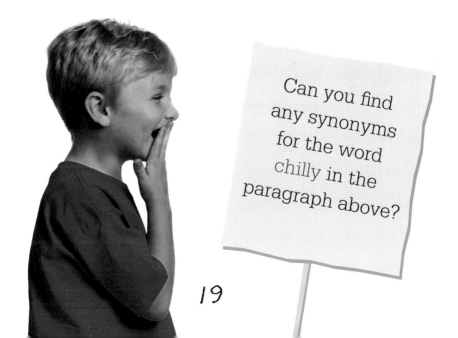

Can you find any synonyms for the word chilly in the paragraph above?

What synonyms can you use to describe the bright leaves?

Glossary

brilliant – very bright.

brisk – cool, fresh, and energizing.

overcast – cloudy.

pleasant – very pleasing.

prefer – to like better or best.

vibrant – a bright shade of a color.

vivid – having very bright colors.

Words I Know

Nouns
A noun is a person, place, or thing.

air, 19
day(s), 5, 13, 15, 17
drizzle, 15
hair, 15
lake, 19
leaves, 20

rainbow, 7
school, 15
sky, 9, 17
streets, 15
sun, 15, 17
synonyms, 20

temperature, 17
umbrella, 13
way, 15
weather, 19
winter, 11, 19

Verbs
A verb is an action or being word.

be, 15
can, 20
describe, 20
does, 15
enjoys, 19

freezes, 19
is, 5, 7, 9, 11, 17, 19
like(s), 15, 19
makes, 15, 17
prefers, 15

skate, 19
skating, 19
turns, 19
use(s), 13, 20
walks, 15

Words I Know

Adjectives
An adjective describes something.

agreeable, 5

beautiful, 17

bright, 7, 15, 17, 20

brilliant, 7

brisk, 11, 19

chilly, 11, 19

clear, 17

cloudy, 9

cold, 11

colorful, 7

cool, 11, 19

damp, 13, 15

foggy, 9

freezing, 11

frizzy, 15

gloomy, 9

good, 5

gray, 9

her, 15

high, 17

lovely, 5, 17

moist, 13

nice, 5

overcast, 9

pleasant, 5, 17

pleasing, 5

rainy, 13, 15

snowy, 11

soggy, 13, 15

stormy, 9

warm, 17

wet, 13

what, 20

vibrant, 7

vivid, 7

Proper Nouns
A proper noun is the name of a person, place, or thing.

Hanna, 15

Kim, 13

Seth, 19

About SandCastle™

A professional team of educators, reading specialists, and content developers created the SandCastle™ series to support young readers as they develop reading skills and strategies and increase their general knowledge. The SandCastle™ series has four levels that correspond to early literacy development in young children. The levels are provided to help teachers and parents select the appropriate books for young readers.

Emerging Readers
(no flags)

Beginning Readers
(1 flag)

Transitional Readers
(2 flags)

Fluent Readers
(3 flags)

These levels are meant only as a guide. All levels are subject to change.

To see a complete list of SandCastle™ books and other nonfiction titles from ABDO Publishing Company, visit www.abdopublishing.com or contact us at: 4940 Viking Drive, Edina, Minnesota 55435 · 1-800-800-1312 · fax: 1-952-831-1632